Gar

TONGUE TWISTERS

By Mark Acey and Scott Nickel

Garfield created by JiM DAViS

LERNER PUBLICATIONS ◆ MINNEAPOLIS

Garfield crunches crunchy crust.

Nickelodeon is a Trademark of Viacom International Inc.

Visit Garfield online at https://www.garfield.com

Lerner Publications Company
An imprint of Lerner Publishing Group, Inc.
241 First Avenue North
Minneapolis, MN 55401 USA

For reading levels and more information, look up this title at www.lernerbooks.com.

Image credit: tashh1601/iStock/Getty Images, p. 9.

Main body text set in Mikado a Bold.
Typeface provided by HVD Fonts.

Designer: Susan Rouleau-Fienhage

Library of Congress Cataloging-in-Publication Data

The Cataloging-in-Publication Data for *Garfield's Tongue Twisters* is on file at the Library of Congress.
ISBN 978-1-5415-8982-7 (lib. bdg.)
ISBN 978-1-72841-348-8 (pbk.)
ISBN 978-1-72840-027-3 (eb pdf)

Manufactured in the United States of America
1-47492-48036-1/9/2020

Crazy clown's crown

Garfield grows greenery.

Garfield dunks doughnuts daily.

DOUGHNUTS AND COFFEE—MEANT TO BE TOGETHER

Twenty tricky
tongue twisters

Garfield gobbles gobs
of goulash.

She saw
Sherri's shoes.

Sheep shorn short
sleep soundly.

Mind-numbing mundane Monday

THE BEST THING TO DO ON A MONDAY: STAY IN BED

Perfect purring Persians

Pepe's peppy puppy pounced.

Funny feline feeling fine

Susie likes to snack on sushi.

A stinky skunk sat on a stump.

A noisy noise annoys an oyster.

Lasagna lovers live longer.

Arlene smiles when she sees cheese.

DIVE INTO YOUR PASSIONS!

Garfield picks pickled peppers off his pepperoni pizza.

JUST GIVE ME PLAIN PEPPERONI, PLEASE

Jon shops for a
sharp shirt.

I wish for
a dish of
delicious
fish.

Toni throws
three free
throws.

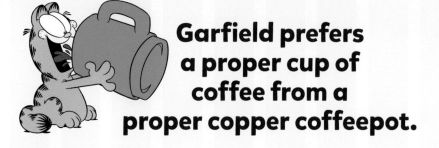

Garfield prefers a proper cup of coffee from a proper copper coffeepot.

THE BIGGER THE CUP, THE BETTER

A cool cat cooks cupcakes quickly.

Drooling dogs drink daily.

Two witches were watching two watches.

Six sticks stacked in six stacks

The famished feline forages for food.

THERE'S NO SUCH THING AS TOO MUCH FOOD

Six sick sheep sleep.

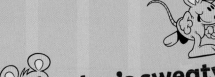

Jon's sweaty socks made Jon's suede shoes smell.

Great grape growers grow great grapes.

15

Jon juggles jelly jars in July.

Garfield chews chunks of chewy cheddar cheese.

EXTRA CHEESE? YES, PLEASE!

Betty's butter is a bit better than her brother Beto's butter.

Odie smelled the smelly sock that smelled smelly.

The llamas' mamas lounge in pajamas.

When it's cold,
Odie's fleas freeze.

I WISH ODIE'S
DROOL WOULD
FREEZE

Garfield feasts on fifty fried fritters.

A baby bunny blew big blue bubbles.

Seven shellfish selfies

Garfield likes lucky lions who lounge lazily.

ANYONE WHO LOUNGES LAZILY IS OK IN MY BOOK

A pussycat pigs out on pasta.

A unique unicorn uses a unique ukulele.

Nine nimble nightingales nibbling nuts

Two tiny toads try to teach two timid turtles to trot.

Beefing up on big, brawny burgers

Katy caught the
kitten in the kitchen.

The kooky cat
craves coffee.

Liz left the lazy lizard
in the loft.

How many cookies could a cooking cat cook if a cooking cat could cook cookies?

Nermal's thermal mittens normally keep Nermal warm.

Slithering snakes slither silently.

The sleepy cat sleeps soundly.

Roxy runs through rural Roman ruins.

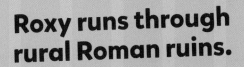

Free fresh fruit from friendly farmers

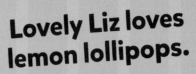

Lovely Liz loves
lemon lollipops.

GOOOOAL!

Garfield goes for
great goals.

Odie chooses
shoes to chew.

Superstar slammer's slam bam funk dunk

Nine nice newts napping nicely

Chewy, chunky chocolate chip cookies

Garfield grabbed the green glue gun.

Roger and Ricki ride rolling red wagons.

HEY, I HAVE NO IDEA WHO ATE ALL THE COOKIES

Fine friends find football fun.

THIS CAT PLAYS TO WIN!

A herd of happy hippos had hiccups.

A big bug bit a bigger bug back.

Beautiful butterflies flutter by.

Six super scoops of ice cream

WHAT'S BETTER THAN A SCOOP OF ICE CREAM? *SIX SCOOPS* OF ICE CREAM!

Eleven eloquent elephants entered the elevator.